AF284001

This igloo book belongs to:

....

igloobooks

Published in 2015
by Igloo Books Ltd
Cottage Farm
Sywell
NN6 0BJ
www.igloobooks.com

HUN001 0515
2 4 6 8 10 9 7 5 3 1
ISBN 978-1-78440-973-9

Written by Melanie Joyce
Illustrated by James Newman Gray
Additional colour by Nigel Chilvers

Printed and manufactured in China

The Magic
Toy Box

igloobooks

The clock struck twelve at Lucy's house and she was fast asleep.
Across the moonlit bedroom floor, shadows began to creep.

A sound came from the toy box. The lid creaked and opened wide.
"It's time to play," whispered Teddy, to all the toys inside.

Lucy was cuddled up in bed,
as snuggly as could be.
So, the toys climbed from the toy box
and shouted out, "Yippee!"

"Shh, now, don't wake Lucy.
Be quiet, you naughty toys.
Bring the disco ball," said Teddy.
"Don't make too much noise."

"Woof-woof," said Puppy, wagging his tail,
sniffing under the bed.
He pulled out the lid of an old board game.
"I've got an idea," he said.

The toys crept into the hall,
so quietly, on tiptoe.
They climbed on board and Puppy said,

"Hold on tight.
Let's go!"

Whoo

They slid down the stairs,
with a bumpety-bump.
Everyone landed,
thumpety-thump.

Teddy opened the living room door.
"Come on," he said. "Let's go.
I've found the perfect place
for a brilliant toy disco."

Soon, the disco ball was glittering.
It swirled and whirled around.

"Everybody dance!" cried Teddy.
"Dig that disco sound!"

Hippo wiggled and Monkey giggled,
as all the toys began to bop.

Singing along, as he danced to the song,
Bunny went hippety-hop!

"Time for a break!" cried Teddy,
as his hungry tummy rumbled.
Into the kitchen, to find some food,
the happy toys all tumbled.

They piled their plates with cookies and cake
and tasty things to eat.

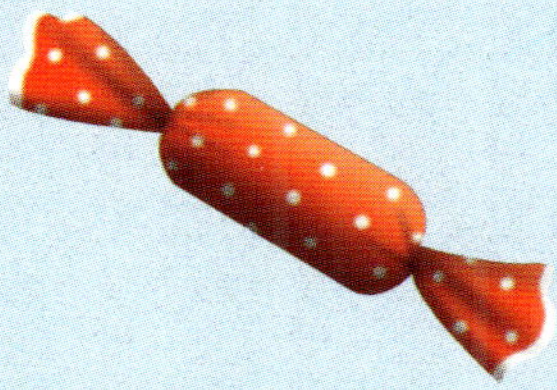

Monkey munched, Croc went crunch
and they gobbled up every treat.

At last the toys were really full
and couldn't eat one bite more.
It was time to tidy up, so
Bunny swept the floor.

Teddy washed the dishes with a
scrub, scrub, scrub.
Puppy dried them off with a
rub, dub, dub.

Outside, the stars were fading
fast and it was nearly dawn.
"Back to the toy box everyone,"
said Teddy, with a yawn.

Up the stairs, the toys all climbed,
as quickly as they could go.
Teddy felt very sleepy,
his little legs started to slow.

"Hurry," whispered Bunny,
as he hopped up into the chest.

"Hey! Wait for me!" cried Teddy,
who had stopped to take a rest.

The toy box lid was closing,
so Teddy lay on the floor.
Soon, he was in a deep sleep
and softly began to snore.

When she woke up in the morning, Lucy stretched and rubbed her eyes.
"How did my bear get over there?" she thought, to her surprise.

"Lovely Bear," said Lucy, as she blinked in the morning light,
"I wonder what you were doing, while I was asleep last night."

What a great party!

Goodbye